The Road Man's Exit Plan: A Guide to Financial Resilience in Uncertain Times

- Understanding your current income, expenses, and debt.
- Building a clear picture of your financial health.

- Creating a realistic budget that reflects your financial reality.
- Identifying areas where you can cut expenses.
- The 50/30/20 rule: Allocating income wisely.

- The importance of an emergency fund.
- How to start and grow your emergency fund.
- What constitutes a financial emergency.

- Strategies for paying down high-interest debt.
- Consolidation options and their pros and cons.
- Avoiding common debt traps.

- The benefits of multiple income streams.
- Identifying opportunities for additional income.
- Balancing side gigs with your primary job.

Introduction

Embarking on a successful financial journey necessitates a solid foundation, and that foundation begins with a thorough comprehension of your current financial standing. This pivotal chapter is your gateway to this essential step in your financial planning journey. Within its pages, we will delve into the intricacies of assessing your financial situation, a process that goes beyond mere number-crunching. Instead, it's about building a comprehensive and accurate snapshot of your financial landscape, which encompasses not only your income and expenses but also a meticulous examination of your debts, assets, and financial goals.

As we navigate through this chapter, you will gain the practical skills and knowledge needed to carry out this assessment effectively. You will learn to scrutinize your income sources, whether they are regular pay checks, side hustles, or investment returns, to create a complete overview of your cash inflow. Simultaneously, we will take a deep dive into your expenses, categorizing them meticulously to distinguish between essential and discretionary spending.

Yet, it doesn't stop there. We will also explore the often-overlooked aspect of debt. By understanding the different types of debt, you may carry, such as mortgages, student loans, or credit card balances, you will gain insight into the financial obligations that may impact your long-term goals.

By the conclusion of this chapter, you will have far more than just a set of numbers. You will possess a realistic and holistic view of your financial health, a starting point from which to make informed financial decisions. This newfound clarity will be the bedrock upon which you construct your financial plan, laying the groundwork for a secure and prosperous financial future.

Chapter 1: Assessing Your Current Financial Situation

Gathering Income Information

Your income forms the basis of your financial well-being, and comprehending its sources is essential for financial stability. Begin by listing all the various sources of income that contribute to your household's finances. These sources may encompass your primary salary or wages, any rental income you receive, earnings from investments like dividends or interest, income generated from side hustles, or government benefits or support you may be eligible for. The collective sum of these income sources is your total monthly income, serving as the starting point for your budgeting and financial planning efforts.

If your income isn't consistent month-to-month, calculate an average monthly income based on the past six months. This approach provides a more stable foundation for budgeting, ensuring that you're not caught off guard during months when income fluctuations occur.

Analyzing Expenses

To establish effective financial planning, it's imperative to discern where your financial resources are being allocated. Start by identifying your fixed expenses—those regular and unchanging costs that comprise the core of your monthly expenditures. This category typically includes payments like rent or mortgage, utility bills (such as electricity, water, and gas), loan repayments (e.g., car loans or student loans), insurance premiums (covering health, car, and home), and recurring subscription services like Netflix or gym memberships.

Variable expenses, on the other hand, fluctuate from month to month and include items like groceries, dining out, transportation expenses (e.g., fuel or public transit fares), entertainment costs, and discretionary shopping. Don't overlook irregular expenses, such as annual insurance premiums, vehicle maintenance, or holiday-related expenditures. To incorporate these irregular costs into your monthly budget, divide their annual total by 12.

Furthermore, categorize your expenses as discretionary (optional) or non-discretionary (essential). This distinction helps identify areas where you may have the flexibility to cut costs when necessary.

Understanding Debt

Debt can significantly impact your financial well-being, making it imperative to be well-informed about your outstanding obligations. Begin by listing all your debts, which may include credit card balances, various loans (personal, auto, student), mortgage or home equity loans, outstanding medical bills, or any other financial obligations.

For each debt, record not only the current balance but also the interest rate attached to it. This information proves vital when devising a strategy to manage and eventually eliminate your debts. Additionally, take note of the minimum monthly payments required for each debt, as failing to meet these obligations can lead to penalties and adversely affect your credit score.

Calculating Your Net Worth

Your net worth serves as a measure of your overall financial health, indicating your financial stability or need for debt reduction. Calculating it involves a simple equation: subtract your total debts from your total assets.

Begin by listing all your assets, which encompass your savings accounts, various investments (such as stocks, bonds, and retirement accounts), real estate holdings (including your home or other properties), vehicles you own, and any personal belongings with significant value. Then, sum up the total value of your assets.

Next, calculate your total debts by adding up all your outstanding financial obligations listed in Section 3. Subtract this debt total from your asset total to find your net worth. A positive net worth signifies financial stability, while a negative net worth signals the need for immediate debt reduction efforts. Your net worth is a benchmark that can track your financial progress over time, helping you make more informed financial decisions.

Assessing your current financial situation is the crucial first step in achieving financial stability. By understanding your income, expenses, debt, and net worth, you gain the knowledge needed to make informed financial decisions. In the following chapters, we'll use this foundation to create a tailored financial plan that aligns with your goals and aspirations. Remember, financial empowerment begins with a clear understanding of your financial health.

Chapter 2: Budgeting for Stability

Creating a Realistic Budget

A budget is the blueprint for your financial well-being, and crafting one that accurately reflects your financial situation is paramount. Begin by tracking all your sources of income. This encompasses your primary salary or wages, earnings from side gigs or investments, rental income, and any other inflow of cash. By compiling this information, you'll have a clear picture of your monthly income, which serves as the foundation for your budget.

Next, list your expenses. Categorize them into three main groups: fixed, variable, and irregular expenses. Fixed expenses are those consistent payments that remain unchanged month after month, including rent or mortgage, utilities, insurance premiums, and loan payments. Variable expenses, on the other hand, fluctuate and include costs like groceries, dining out, entertainment, and transportation. Irregular expenses may not occur monthly but still impact your finances, such as annual insurance premiums or holiday expenses.

Calculate your savings goals and allocate a portion of your income to savings as a non-negotiable expense. This step is vital for building financial security and achieving your long-term financial objectives. Finally, calculate the difference between your total income and total expenses (including savings). A positive balance signifies that you're living within your means, while a negative balance may indicate the need to make adjustments to your spending habits.

Identifying Expense Reduction Opportunities

Budgeting isn't solely about tracking expenses; it's also about finding opportunities to cut costs and redirect those savings towards your financial goals. Begin by reviewing your variable and discretionary expenses. Consider whether there are areas where you can trim expenditures. Perhaps you can reduce dining out by cooking at home more frequently or explore more affordable transportation options.

Don't overlook opportunities to negotiate fixed expenses. Shop around for better insurance rates, reach out to service providers to renegotiate bills like cable or internet, or explore loan refinancing options to secure lower interest rates. Additionally, eliminate unnecessary subscriptions and memberships that may be draining your budget. This could involve cancelling underutilized streaming services, gym memberships, or magazine subscriptions. Lastly, consider bulk shopping and discounts to save on essential items, as even small savings on everyday purchases can accumulate significantly over time.

The 50/30/20 Rule: Allocating Income Wisely

The 50/30/20 rule provides a balanced framework for allocating your income to ensure financial stability and flexibility. Approximately 50% of your income should be earmarked for essential needs. These are the non-negotiable expenses that encompass housing, utilities, groceries, transportation, insurance, and minimum debt payments. Keeping these costs within the 50% threshold is crucial to maintaining financial stability.

Allocate about 30% of your income to discretionary spending and wants. This category covers expenses related to dining out, entertainment, hobbies, and non-essential purchases. It allows room for flexibility and enjoyment in your budget without jeopardizing your financial security.

Dedicate a minimum of 20% of your income to savings and debt repayment. This portion plays a critical role in building an emergency fund, contributing to retirement accounts, and paying off high-interest debts. If possible, strive to increase this allocation to expedite your progress towards achieving your financial goals.

Maintaining and Adjusting Your Budget

A budget is not a one-time task but an ongoing process that requires regular attention. Periodically review and adjust your budget to ensure it remains aligned with your financial goals and evolving circumstances. Major life changes, such as a new job, marriage, or the birth of a child, can impact your income and expenses. When such changes occur, update your budget accordingly to accommodate them.

Budgeting apps and online tools can simplify this process by automating expense tracking and providing real-time insights into your financial health. By consistently monitoring and adjusting your budget as needed, you'll be well-equipped to make informed financial decisions, achieve your goals, and maintain a healthy financial life. Remember, your budget is a dynamic tool that can adapt to your changing financial landscape.

Creating and maintaining a realistic budget is the cornerstone of financial stability. It allows you to manage your income effectively, identify areas for cost-cutting, and allocate your resources wisely according to the 50/30/20 rule. By following the guidelines outlined in this chapter, you'll be well-equipped to take control of your finances, achieve your financial goals, and build a strong foundation for financial stability. Remember that a well-managed budget is a powerful tool for financial success.

Chapter 3: Emergency Fund Essentials

Understanding the Importance of an Emergency Fund

An emergency fund is a financial lifeline that should be a cornerstone of your financial plan. Its significance cannot be overstated, as it serves as your buffer against unexpected financial shocks. These shocks can come in many forms, such as medical emergencies, car breakdowns, sudden job loss, or home repairs. Without an emergency fund, you may find yourself forced to rely on high-interest credit cards or loans to cover these expenses, potentially plunging you into a cycle of debt that can be challenging to escape.

Moreover, the financial security an emergency fund provides is invaluable. Knowing that you have a safety net in place can alleviate a significant amount of stress and anxiety when faced with unexpected financial challenges. It allows you to approach these situations with a clear mind and a sense of control, as you won't be scrambling to find quick solutions or borrowing at exorbitant interest rates. In essence, an emergency fund is your shield against financial turmoil and an essential component of a solid financial foundation.

Starting and Growing Your Emergency Fund

Building an emergency fund is a gradual process that requires a strategic approach. Begin by setting clear financial goals for your fund. Consider factors like your monthly living expenses, the stability of your income, and the nature of potential emergencies you may face. While a common guideline suggests saving three to six months' worth of living expenses, your specific circumstances and comfort level may lead you to a different target.

Once you have a goal in mind, create a dedicated savings account for your emergency fund. This separation helps prevent you from dipping into the fund for non-emergencies. Start small if necessary, contributing what you can comfortably afford. The key is consistency. Set up automatic transfers from your main account to your emergency fund to ensure regular contributions, even if they are relatively modest at first.

As your financial situation improves, aim to increase your contributions over time. Windfalls and unexpected bonuses can also provide opportunities to give your emergency fund a boost. Remember that the growth of your emergency fund is a journey that takes time and discipline, so be patient and persistent.

What Constitutes a Financial Emergency

Not every unexpected expense qualifies as a genuine financial emergency. It's essential to differentiate between situations that warrant tapping into your emergency fund and those that should be covered by your regular budget.

A genuine financial emergency typically involves situations like unforeseen medical expenses, sudden job loss, essential vehicle or home repairs, or unexpected travel due to family emergencies. These are events that can significantly disrupt your financial stability and require immediate attention.

On the other hand, non-emergencies encompass regular bills like rent or utilities, discretionary spending such as dining out or entertainment, and expected costs like annual insurance premiums or holiday expenses. These expenses should be factored into your monthly budget and not funded by your emergency fund.

Being discerning about what constitutes a financial emergency ensures that your emergency fund remains intact and available when you truly need it most, safeguarding your financial well-being during unforeseen challenges.

An emergency fund isn't just a financial tool; it's your lifeline in times of unexpected turmoil. Its importance lies in its ability to provide financial security, prevent debt, and reduce stress during difficult circumstances. By grasping its significance, setting clear goals, and systematically growing your fund, you can establish a robust financial safety net. Furthermore, distinguishing between genuine emergencies and regular expenses ensures that your emergency fund remains accessible when faced with unexpected financial challenges. Ultimately, an emergency fund is an essential pillar of financial preparedness, granting you the confidence and resilience to face life's uncertainties head-on.

Chapter 4: Debt Management Strategies

Strategies for Paying Down High-Interest Debt

High-interest debt can be a financial obstacle that prevents you from achieving your financial goals. Prioritizing high-interest debts is the first step in taking control of your financial situation. Start by identifying which debts carry the highest annual percentage rates (APRs) – typically credit card balances or personal loans. These are the debts that cost you the most in interest charges over time.

Once you've identified your high-interest debts, create a structured debt repayment plan. There are two popular methods to consider: the snowball method and the avalanche method. The snowball method involves paying off the smallest debts first, which can provide a psychological boost as you quickly see progress. The avalanche method prioritizes paying off debts with the highest interest rates, which saves you more money in interest charges in the long run. Choose the approach that aligns with your financial situation and motivates you to make consistent payments.

Increasing your monthly payments beyond the minimum is essential for accelerating debt reduction. Even small additional payments can add up and help you become debt-free sooner. Additionally, consider negotiating with your creditors for lower interest rates. A reduced rate can make it easier to pay off your debt faster, so it's worth exploring.

Whenever you receive unexpected windfalls, such as tax refunds or work bonuses, consider allocating a portion or the entirety of these funds toward your high-interest debt. These lump-sum payments can make a significant impact on reducing your outstanding balances.

Debt Consolidation Options and Their Pros and Cons

Debt consolidation can be a valuable tool for simplifying your debt management and potentially reducing interest costs. It's crucial to understand the various methods and their pros and cons.

Balance transfer credit cards can be advantageous because they often offer low or 0% introductory APRs for a specific period. This allows you to consolidate multiple high-interest credit card balances into one, potentially saving on interest. However, be aware that introductory rates expire, and higher rates may apply afterward, and balance transfer fees may be imposed.

Personal loans offer the benefit of fixed interest rates and predictable monthly payments. They can be used to consolidate various types of debt, providing flexibility. Nevertheless, interest rates for unsecured personal loans may be higher, and approval may depend on your creditworthiness.

Debt consolidation loans are designed specifically for consolidating multiple debts into a single loan, potentially offering competitive interest rates, particularly if collateral is involved. However, there is a risk of losing collateral if you're unable to repay, and eligibility and rates can vary based on credit and collateral.

Debt management plans (DMPs) are structured plans for repaying unsecured debts. They may negotiate lower interest rates and fees with creditors, making repayment more manageable. However, enrolling in a DMP typically requires working with a credit counselling agency, and it may not cover secured debts like mortgages.

Avoiding Common Debt Traps

Effectively managing debt isn't just about paying it off; it also involves avoiding common pitfalls that can lead to increased debt or financial instability.

One key strategy is to minimize credit card usage for non-essential expenses. Overreliance on credit for everyday purchases can lead to increased debt, especially if you only make minimum payments.

Maintaining a well-funded emergency fund is another essential component of responsible financial management. Having this fund in place helps you cover unexpected expenses without resorting to credit, reducing the need for additional debt.

Budgeting diligently is fundamental to debt avoidance. Creating and adhering to a comprehensive budget that accounts for all your expenses, including debt repayments, ensures you stay on track and avoid accumulating more debt.

Sometimes, making temporary lifestyle adjustments can significantly impact your ability to repay debt. Reducing discretionary spending and reallocating those funds toward debt repayment can expedite your journey to becoming debt-free.

Finally, don't hesitate to seek professional guidance if your debt situation becomes unmanageable. Reputable credit counselling agencies and financial advisors can provide tailored advice and strategies to help you regain control of your finances.

Debt management is a crucial aspect of achieving financial stability. By prioritizing high-interest debt, creating a structured repayment plan, and exploring consolidation options, you can make significant progress in reducing your debt burden. However, it's equally important to avoid common debt traps by practicing responsible credit card usage, maintaining an emergency fund, budgeting diligently, making lifestyle adjustments when necessary, and seeking professional guidance when facing overwhelming debt. Successfully managing and reducing your debt will not only improve your financial health but also provide peace of mind and open the door to a more secure financial future.

Chapter 5: Income Diversification

The Benefits of Multiple Income Streams

Depending solely on one source of income is like building a house on a single pillar; it can be precarious. The concept of income diversification revolves around the idea of constructing a stable financial foundation by creating multiple streams of income. The advantages of adopting this approach are multifaceted:

Firstly, it grants you financial resilience. Life is unpredictable and relying on one income source leaves you vulnerable to unexpected circumstances such as job loss or economic downturns. When you diversify your income, disruptions in one area can be compensated for by the others, safeguarding your financial stability.

Secondly, income diversification provides the means for enhanced savings and investments. With more money flowing in from various sources, you have the capacity to accelerate your progress toward critical financial goals, be it building an emergency fund, investing for retirement, or achieving other aspirations.

Furthermore, this approach reduces financial stress. It redistributes the weight of covering expenses across multiple income streams, lessening the pressure on any single source. As a result, you're more likely to feel secure about your financial situation and be better equipped to deal with financial challenges.

Lastly, income diversification opens the door to opportunities for personal and professional growth. Side gigs, investments, or entrepreneurial ventures started as supplementary income sources can evolve into full-fledged careers or substantial financial successes over time, unlocking new horizons and ambitions.

Identifying Opportunities for Additional Income

The journey to income diversification begins with identifying opportunities that align with your skills, interests, and available time. Here's how to spot potential sources of supplementary income:

Exploring side gigs is often a great starting point. These can encompass a wide range of freelance work or part-time jobs, depending on your expertise and interests. Whether it's consulting, tutoring, writing, or participating in the gig economy, there are numerous avenues to explore.

Investing wisely is another avenue. Stocks, bonds, real estate, and other assets have the potential to generate passive income through dividends, interest, or rental income. However, it's crucial to comprehend the risks and rewards associated with each investment type before committing.

For those with an entrepreneurial spirit, starting a small business or launching an online venture can yield substantial returns. Evaluate your business ideas carefully and be prepared to invest the time and resources required for success.

Rental income can also be a viable option if you have extra space. Platforms like Airbnb or traditional long-term rentals can provide a consistent and relatively passive source of income.

Passive income streams offer a more hands-off approach. These may include creating and selling digital products, writing a book, or developing an online course. Once established, these income sources require less ongoing effort, making them attractive options.

Balancing Side Gigs with Your Primary Job

Effectively balancing multiple income streams, especially when you have a primary job, necessitates astute time management and prioritization:

Time management plays a pivotal role. Carefully plan your schedule to accommodate both your primary job and side gigs. Employ calendars and productivity tools to stay organized and ensure you meet all your commitments.

Prioritization is key. Determine which income streams are most critical and allocate your time and energy accordingly. Your primary job may take precedence, but it's vital to set aside sufficient time to nurture and grow your side gigs.

Set realistic goals for each income stream, including financial targets and time commitments. This prevents burnout and ensures a balanced approach to your work.

Flexibility is crucial. Be adaptable and open to adjusting your schedule as needed. Unexpected work demands or personal commitments may require shifting priorities temporarily.

Lastly, don't forget self-care. Maintaining a healthy work-life balance is vital for long-term sustainability. Avoid overextending yourself and remember that your physical and mental well-being are paramount.

Income diversification is a robust financial strategy that offers resilience, growth opportunities, and reduced stress. By exploring various income sources such as side gigs, investments, entrepreneurship, or passive income streams, you can create a more secure financial future. Nevertheless, achieving a harmonious balance between these income streams and your primary job necessitates effective time management, prioritization, and self-care to ensure sustained success. Embracing income diversification not only enhances your financial stability but also provides the flexibility to pursue your financial goals with confidence. It's a dynamic approach that can yield enduring benefits for your financial well-being.

Chapter 6: Investments and Savings

Investment Options for All Investors

Investing is a crucial pathway to building wealth, and it's accessible to individuals at all levels of experience. For beginners, it's advisable to start with low-risk investments that provide a gentle introduction to the world of finance. Savings accounts and Certificates of Deposit (CDs) are safe options, ideal for those who prioritize capital preservation. They offer modest interest rates and are highly liquid, ensuring that your money remains easily accessible.

Moving a step further, stock market index funds present an excellent entry point into the world of equities. These funds pool money from multiple investors and offer broad exposure to the stock market. They are a straightforward choice for beginners, as they provide instant diversification without the need for in-depth stock analysis.

Bonds are another option, offering relative stability and regular interest payments. These fixed-income securities are less volatile than stocks, making them suitable for conservative investors.

For those looking for more flexibility and diversification, Exchange-Traded Funds (ETFs) are an excellent choice. Similar to index funds, they offer exposure to a variety of assets but can be traded like individual stocks. This versatility makes them appealing to both beginners and experienced investors, as they can tailor their portfolios to specific sectors or investment themes.

For more experienced investors, the universe of investment choices expands. Individual stocks offer the potential for substantial returns but require in-depth research and analysis. Real estate, whether through direct property ownership or real estate investment trusts (REITs), provides exposure to a tangible asset class with potential for rental income and property appreciation. Mutual funds managed by professionals can cater to those looking for expert guidance and a diversified portfolio tailored to specific investment goals.

The Power of Compounding and Long-Term Savings

Understanding the power of compounding is akin to unlocking the secret to long-term financial growth. This concept emphasizes that not only does your initial investment grow over time, but the returns on your investment also generate additional returns.

Starting early is critical to harnessing the full potential of compounding. Even small, consistent contributions to your savings and investment accounts can lead to substantial wealth accumulation when given enough time to grow. The sooner you begin, the more time your money has to work for you.

Consistency plays a vital role in compounding. Automating your contributions ensures that you continue to invest regularly, regardless of market fluctuations or economic conditions. Even during periods of market volatility, maintaining a steady savings and investment routine can pay significant dividends in the long run.

Reinvesting returns is another essential aspect of compounding. Rather than withdrawing interest, dividends, or capital gains, allow these earnings to remain in your investments. Over time, this reinvestment can lead to exponential growth, significantly amplifying the value of your portfolio.

Finally, a long-term perspective is fundamental to the power of compounding. Investors who focus on their long-term financial goals and resist reacting to short-term market volatility are better positioned to benefit from the full potential of this wealth-building concept.

Risk Tolerance and Asset Allocation

Navigating the world of investments requires an understanding of your risk tolerance and thoughtful asset allocation:

Assessing your risk tolerance is the first step. Consider factors like your financial goals, time horizon, and comfort level with market fluctuations. Are you willing to accept higher volatility in exchange for potentially higher returns, or do you prefer a more conservative approach that prioritizes capital preservation and stability?

Asset allocation involves the strategic distribution of your investments across different asset classes, such as stocks, bonds, and cash equivalents. The allocation should reflect your risk tolerance and financial objectives. Younger investors with a longer time horizon may opt for a more aggressive allocation with a higher proportion of stocks to pursue growth. In contrast, those nearing retirement may favour a more conservative mix to protect their capital.

Diversification is a critical component of risk management. Within each asset class, spreading your investments across various industries, regions, and sectors can reduce the impact of a poorly performing investment on your overall portfolio. Diversification helps mitigate risk while still allowing you to benefit from potential opportunities in different segments of the market.

Regularly reviewing your investment portfolio and adjusting your asset allocation is essential. Over time, your circumstances may change, and your risk tolerance may evolve. Periodic rebalancing ensures that your investments remain aligned with your goals and risk tolerance, helping you stay on track to achieve your financial objectives.

Investments and savings are integral elements of financial success, and they cater to individuals at various experience levels. Understanding the investment options available, the power of compounding, and the importance of long-term savings sets the stage for building wealth over time. Additionally, assessing your risk tolerance and strategically allocating your assets are crucial steps in constructing a well-balanced and resilient investment portfolio. By incorporating these principles into your financial strategy, you can work toward securing a prosperous and financially stable future.

Chapter 7: Insurance and Risk Mitigation

The Role of Insurance in Financial Protection

Insurance serves as an essential financial safety net, shielding individuals and families from the potentially devastating impact of unforeseen events. At its core, insurance is a risk mitigation strategy that transfers the financial burden of unexpected situations to an insurance provider. These situations can range from health issues and accidents to disability, property damage, or even the loss of a primary breadwinner. By taking out insurance policies, individuals protect their hard-earned assets and ensure they have a financial cushion to fall back on when life takes an unexpected turn.

Beyond financial protection, insurance provides peace of mind. Knowing that you have insurance coverage in place alleviates stress and anxiety, allowing you to focus on your life goals and aspirations with confidence. It acts as a critical layer of financial security, preventing you from being overwhelmed by burdensome medical bills, repair costs, or other unexpected expenses. Furthermore, in many cases, insurance isn't just a prudent choice; it's a legal or contractual requirement. Failure to meet these requirements can result in legal consequences and financial liabilities, emphasizing its importance in safeguarding your financial well-being.

Types of Insurance to Consider

Various types of insurance cater to different aspects of risk and financial protection. Health insurance, for instance, is indispensable for covering medical expenses, ensuring that you can access healthcare services without facing exorbitant out-of-pocket costs. Understanding the specifics of your health insurance policy, including coverage, co-payments, and deductibles, is essential for making informed healthcare decisions.

Disability insurance steps in to replace a portion of your income should you become unable to work due to illness or injury. It offers critical financial support during periods of disability, allowing you to meet your financial obligations and maintain your standard of living.

Life insurance, on the other hand, is designed to provide financial security to your loved ones in the event of your passing. It offers a death benefit to your beneficiaries, helping them cover expenses like funeral costs, outstanding debts, and ongoing living expenses. With various forms of life insurance available, such as term life and whole life, it's crucial to choose the one that aligns with your unique financial goals.

Property insurance, including homeowners' and renters' insurance, safeguards your property against damage or loss caused by events like fires, natural disasters, theft, or vandalism. Understanding the specific coverage, deductibles, and limits of your property insurance policies is essential to ensure that your assets are adequately protected.

Auto insurance, often mandated by law, provides coverage for accidents, vehicle damage, liability, and medical expenses arising from car accidents. Selecting the right coverage levels and deductibles based on your needs and budget is critical for responsible vehicle ownership.

Understanding Deductibles and Coverage Limits

To make the most of your insurance policies, it's crucial to grasp key concepts like deductibles and coverage limits. Deductibles represent the amount you must pay out of pocket before your insurance coverage takes effect. For instance, if you have a $1,000 deductible on your auto insurance policy and incur $3,000 in repair costs after an accident, you will pay the initial $1,000, and your insurance provider would cover the remaining $2,000. Opting for higher deductibles often leads to lower insurance premiums but requires you to bear more of the initial expense in the event of a claim.

Coverage limits, on the other hand, determine the maximum amount an insurance policy will pay for a covered claim. For example, if you possess $100,000 in liability coverage on your homeowners' insurance and face liability for $150,000 in damages due to an injury on your property, your insurance will cover the first $100,000, and you would be responsible for the remaining $50,000. Regularly reviewing your policy limits ensures they align with your financial needs and potential risks, preventing underinsurance or over insurance scenarios.

Insurance is an integral part of responsible financial planning and risk management. It plays a pivotal role in shielding your financial well-being, providing peace of mind, and ensuring that unexpected life events don't derail your financial goals. Recognizing the diverse types of insurance available, from health and disability to life and property insurance, empowers you to make informed decisions tailored to your specific needs. Moreover, comprehending essential concepts like deductibles and coverage limits allows you to fine-tune your insurance policies to align with your budget and risk tolerance. By embracing insurance as a fundamental element of your financial strategy, you enhance your financial security and prepare for life's uncertainties with confidence.

Chapter 8: Building a Financial Safety Net

Strategies for Building Long-Term Financial Security

Building a robust financial safety net requires a strategic approach that combines careful planning and disciplined execution. The first step in this journey is establishing clear financial goals. By defining your objectives, whether they involve buying a home, funding your children's education, or securing a comfortable retirement, you create a roadmap for your financial future.

Budgeting and saving are foundational practices. Crafting a realistic budget that outlines your income, expenses, and savings goals enables you to understand your financial picture. Consistently setting aside a portion of your income for savings is crucial for building long-term financial security. Automating your savings ensures that you stay committed to your goals and minimizes the temptation to overspend.

An emergency fund acts as a vital financial cushion. Accumulating at least three to six months' worth of living expenses in this fund provides protection against unforeseen events, such as medical emergencies, job loss, or unexpected repairs. It allows you to weather financial storms without resorting to debt.

Effective debt management is another crucial aspect of financial security. Prioritizing the repayment of high-interest debt reduces financial stress and frees up more of your income for saving and investing. Reducing and ultimately eliminating debt not only provides peace of mind but also accelerates your journey toward financial independence.

Diversifying your investments is key to long-term wealth-building. Constructing a well-balanced investment portfolio that includes a mix of stocks, bonds, real estate, and other assets aligns with your risk tolerance and financial objectives. Regularly reviewing and adjusting your investments ensures that your portfolio remains in line with your goals.

Retirement Planning and Pension Considerations

Planning for retirement is an integral part of securing your long-term financial future. To embark on this journey, start by defining your retirement goals. Consider your desired retirement lifestyle, including expenses, travel plans, and leisure activities. Having a clear vision of your retirement helps estimate how much you need to save.

Retirement accounts play a pivotal role in your financial strategy. Maximize your contributions to retirement vehicles such as 401(k)s, IRAs, or employer-sponsored pension plans. Employer matching contributions represent free money that can significantly boost your retirement savings. Understand the specific rules and benefits of each account to optimize your contributions.

If your employer offers a pension plan, familiarize yourself with its terms and benefits. Pension plans can provide a stable source of retirement income, and understanding how they work is crucial for maximizing your retirement security.

Social Security benefits also play a role in retirement planning. Research the Social Security system to understand the benefits you can expect to receive. Be mindful of the implications of when you choose to begin receiving benefits, as this timing can impact the amount you receive each month.

Consider seeking professional guidance for retirement planning. Financial advisors or retirement planners can help you create a tailored retirement strategy based on your unique circumstances. They provide insights into complex retirement decisions and help you optimize your savings.

Wealth-Building Through Smart Financial Decisions

Wealth-building involves a series of well-informed financial decisions that gradually grow your net worth. Education and skill development are critical components of this journey. Investing in your education and acquiring new skills can increase your earning potential, leading to higher income over time.

Smart tax planning is essential for preserving your wealth. Understanding the tax implications of your financial decisions and exploring tax-efficient strategies for saving and investing can minimize the impact of taxes on your wealth. By making informed choices, you can retain more of your hard-earned money.

Estate planning is another key aspect of wealth-building. Creating a comprehensive estate plan that includes wills, trusts, and powers of attorney ensures that your assets are distributed according to your wishes. Proper estate planning also minimizes potential conflicts among heirs, preserving family harmony.

Consider incorporating philanthropy into your financial plan. Charitable giving not only benefits society but can also have tax advantages and provide personal fulfilment. Giving back to your community or supporting causes you're passionate about can be an integral part of your wealth-building journey.

A long-term financial review is essential for adapting to changing circumstances. Regularly assess your financial plan and make adjustments as necessary. Life is dynamic, and your financial strategy should evolve to address new goals, challenges, and opportunities.

Building a comprehensive financial safety net involves a combination of strategic practices, retirement planning, and intelligent wealth-building decisions. Clear financial goals, budgeting, savings, emergency funds, and debt management set the foundation for your financial security. Retirement planning ensures a comfortable and worry-free retirement, while smart financial decisions, including tax planning, estate planning, and philanthropy, contribute to long-term wealth growth. Continually reviewing and adapting your financial plan ensures that you remain on track to achieve lasting financial stability for yourself and future generations.

Chapter 9: Navigating Income Drops

Coping with Job Loss or Reduced Income

Experiencing a sudden drop in income, whether due to job loss or reduced earnings, is a deeply challenging experience both emotionally and financially. It's essential to approach this situation with a combination of emotional resilience and practicality. Emotionally, it's crucial to acknowledge the impact such an event can have on your mental well-being. Feelings of shock, anxiety, and frustration are entirely normal reactions. Seeking support from friends, family, or a mental health professional can provide a valuable outlet for processing these emotions.

Simultaneously, a thorough assessment of your financial situation is imperative. This includes taking stock of your current financial assets, outstanding debts, and monthly expenses. This assessment provides clarity on your immediate financial needs and sets the stage for crafting a plan to weather the storm.

Creating a revised budget is the next critical step. Your new budget should align with your adjusted income reality. Prioritize essential expenses like housing, utilities, groceries, and insurance while temporarily reducing or eliminating discretionary spending. This revised budget will act as a financial lifeline during the initial phase of income adjustment.

Furthermore, exploring alternative income sources becomes paramount. Whether through part-time work, freelancing, or gig economy opportunities, diversifying your income streams can provide much-needed stability during income fluctuations. Being open to new opportunities and adaptable in your approach to income generation is key during this period.

Steps to Take Immediately After a Sudden Income Drop

In the face of a sudden income drop, taking swift and strategic action is essential to regain control of your financial situation and minimize long-term impact. The first immediate step is to reach out to creditors, lenders, and service providers. Engage in open and honest communication about your circumstances. Many institutions offer temporary relief options, such as deferred payments or modified repayment plans, during times of financial hardship.

Simultaneously, it's crucial to review government assistance programs available to you. These programs can provide critical support during challenging times. Applying for unemployment benefits, if you've lost your job, is a top priority. These benefits are designed to offer temporary financial assistance while you actively seek new employment.

As part of your immediate action plan, re-evaluate your financial goals. Consider postponing non-essential financial objectives until your financial stability is restored. This adjustment may include delaying major purchases, travel plans, or large investments. Ensuring that your short-term financial focus is on stability and essentials is vital during this phase.

Additionally, if you have an emergency fund, consider its judicious utilization to cover necessary expenses. While an emergency fund is intended to serve as a safety net for unexpected emergencies, a sudden income drop qualifies as a legitimate use. However, use caution and only withdraw funds as necessary to cover essential expenses.

Leveraging Government Assistance Programs

Government assistance programs can provide essential support during periods of income uncertainty. Understanding the available options is crucial:

Unemployment benefits should be pursued if you've lost your job or experienced a substantial reduction in income. These benefits offer financial assistance while you actively seek new employment. The application process can vary by location, so be sure to research and follow the guidelines in your region.

Food assistance programs, such as the Supplemental Nutrition Assistance Program (SNAP) in the United States, can help cover the cost of groceries and essential nutrition during challenging times. These programs are designed to ensure that individuals and families have access to sufficient food.

Housing assistance programs and rental assistance options may be available through local or national agencies. These programs aim to alleviate housing-related financial burdens, including rent and mortgage payments.

Healthcare subsidies and options, such as Medicaid or the Affordable Care Act (ACA) marketplaces, can provide access to healthcare coverage if you've lost employer-sponsored healthcare due to an income drop. Maintaining health coverage is essential, and these programs can help bridge the gap.

Debt relief programs or initiatives may offer various forms of assistance, including debt consolidation, loan forgiveness, or reduced interest rates. These measures can help ease financial pressure and provide relief from debt-related burdens.

Navigating a sudden income drop requires a combination of emotional resilience, proactive financial strategies, and a keen understanding of available resources. Coping with the emotional impact while implementing practical measures, such as revising your budget and exploring alternative income sources, is essential for stability. Government assistance programs can provide vital support during challenging times, serving as a temporary safety net until financial stability is regained. Remember that adaptability, resourcefulness, and a proactive approach are key to overcoming income setbacks and building a more secure financial future.

Chapter 10: Staying Resilient and Adapting

The Importance of Adaptability in Financial Planning

Adaptability is the cornerstone of a resilient and effective financial plan. In the ever-changing landscape of personal finance, the ability to respond to shifting circumstances is paramount. Financial plans that rigidly adhere to a single course of action can quickly become obsolete when life takes unexpected turns. Therefore, embracing adaptability is essential for long-term financial well-being.

Life, by its very nature, is unpredictable. Challenges, opportunities, and curveballs are inevitable. An adaptable financial plan acts as a robust framework that can pivot and adjust in response to these changing circumstances. Whether it's a sudden job loss, a medical emergency, or a global economic crisis, adaptability allows you to weather these storms and remain on course toward your financial goals.

Furthermore, economic conditions are dynamic, and financial markets fluctuate over time. Interest rates, inflation, and investment returns are all subject to change. An adaptable financial plan enables you to adjust your investment strategy, spending habits, and savings goals to effectively respond to these shifts. By embracing adaptability, you can navigate these economic fluctuations with confidence.

Adaptability also accommodates personal growth. As you evolve and your life journey unfolds, so do your financial aspirations. What may have been a priority in your 20s may not hold the same significance in your 40s or 50s. An adaptable financial plan empowers you to align your financial goals with your changing values, priorities, and life stages. It enables you to pursue new opportunities and revisit your goals as you progress through different phases of life.

Additionally, financial setbacks are a natural part of one's financial journey. These setbacks could manifest as job loss, health crises, or unexpected expenses. However, an adaptable plan incorporates contingencies and strategies to cope with these setbacks while minimizing their impact on your overall financial stability. Ultimately, adaptability in financial planning ensures that your path to financial success is not hindered by the inevitable challenges that life throws your way.

Learning from Setbacks and Failures

Setbacks and financial failures are not indicative of defeat but rather opportunities for growth and resilience. Adopting a growth mindset is essential when facing financial challenges. Viewing setbacks as learning experiences rather than insurmountable obstacles can provide a more constructive perspective.

When encountering a financial setback, it's vital to analyze the root causes. Understanding why a setback occurred—whether it was due to overspending, inadequate savings, or an unexpected event—provides valuable insights. These insights can help you devise effective strategies to prevent a recurrence. By pinpointing the underlying issues, you can create a more robust financial plan that addresses vulnerabilities and safeguards against future setbacks.

Adjusting your financial approach in response to setbacks is a proactive step toward financial resilience. This adjustment might involve revising your budget, diversifying your investments, or exploring new income opportunities. Each setback offers a chance to refine your financial strategy and implement measures that enhance your financial stability.

Furthermore, building financial resilience is critical. This involves fortifying your financial safety net, including emergency funds and insurance coverage, to better withstand future setbacks. By learning from setbacks and failures, you not only strengthen your financial plan but also cultivate the resilience needed to navigate future challenges with greater confidence.

Setting New Financial Goals and Reassessing Your Plan

Adaptability in financial planning extends to setting new goals and periodically reassessing your financial plan:

Re-evaluating your priorities is a fundamental aspect of adaptability. Life is dynamic, and your values and goals may shift over time. By periodically reassessing what truly matters to you and how your financial goals align with these values, you can ensure that your financial plan remains meaningful and relevant.

Setting new milestones is an essential part of staying adaptable and motivated. As you achieve financial goals, it's crucial to establish new objectives that challenge you and keep your financial journey engaging. Whether it's saving for a dream vacation, starting a business, or funding your children's education, these new goals provide direction and purpose.

Flexibility in your timeline is key. Some financial goals may take longer to achieve than initially expected, while others may become more attainable sooner. Adapting your plan to accommodate changes in your timeline ensures that you remain on track and motivated, regardless of the pace of progress.

Seeking professional guidance periodically is a wise choice. Financial advisors can provide valuable insights, expertise, and objective assessments to help you adjust your plan based on your evolving circumstances and goals. Their input can help you make informed decisions as you navigate changes in your financial life.

Adaptability is not merely a survival strategy in financial planning; it's the key to sustained success and fulfilment. Recognizing the importance of adaptability in navigating life's uncertainties, economic shifts, and personal growth is vital. Setbacks and failures are opportunities for learning and growth, providing valuable lessons that can strengthen your financial plan and enhance your resilience.

Periodically reassessing your financial goals and priorities, setting new milestones, and remaining flexible in your timeline ensures that your financial journey remains aligned with your evolving life circumstances and aspirations. By embracing adaptability and resilience, you can confidently face the challenges and opportunities that lie ahead on your financial path, ultimately achieving a more secure and fulfilling financial future.

"The Road Man's Exit Plan" serves as your comprehensive guide to achieving financial resilience and stability in an increasingly unpredictable world. This book lays out a strategic roadmap, equipping you with the necessary tools and insights to not only navigate sudden income drops effectively but also to thrive amidst ever-evolving circumstances. It underscores the fact that financial planning is not a one-time event but an ongoing, dynamic process. As you immerse yourself in the principles and strategies detailed in these pages, you'll be empowered to seize control of your financial destiny, even in the face of unexpected challenges. By diligently preparing, resiliently persevering, and strategically prospering, you will discover that your financial well-being is not an elusive dream but a tangible and achievable reality well within your grasp.